SONGS OF SUNRISE LANDS

BY

CLINTON SCOLLARD

BOSTON AND NEW YORK
HOUGHTON, MIFFLIN AND
COMPANY. MDCCCXCII

The Riverside Press, Cambridge, Mass., U. S. A.
Electrotyped and Printed by H. O. Houghton & Co.

TO GEORGIA

CONTENTS

KHAMSIN

OH, the wind from the desert blew in! —
Khamsin,
The wind from the desert, blew in!
It blew from the heart of the fiery south,
From the fervid sand and the hills of drouth,
And it kissed the land with its scorching mouth;
The wind from the desert blew in!

It blasted the buds on the almond bough,
And shriveled the fruit on the orange-tree;
The wizened dervish breathed no vow,
So weary and parched was he.
The lean muezzin could not cry;
The dogs ran mad, and bayed the sky;
The hot sun shone like a copper disk,
And prone in the shade of an obelisk
The water-carrier sank with a sigh,

For limp and dry was his water-skin ;
And the wind from the desert blew in.

The camel crouched by the crumbling wall,
And oh, the pitiful moan it made !
The minarets, taper and slim and tall,
Reeled and swam in the brazen light ;
And prayers went up by day and night,
But thin and drawn were the lips that prayed.
The river writhed in its slimy bed,
Shrunk to a tortuous, turbid thread ;
The burnt earth cracked like a cloven rind ;
And still the wind, the ruthless wind,
Khamsin,
The wind from the desert, blew in.

Into the cool of the mosque it crept,
Where the poor sought rest at the Prophet's shrine ;
Its breath was fire to the jasmine vine ;
It fevered the brow of the maid who slept,
And men grew haggard with revel of wine.
The tiny fledgelings died in the nest ;
The sick babe gasped at the mother's breast.
Then a rumor rose and swelled and spread

From a tremulous whisper, faint and vague,
Till it burst in a terrible cry of dread,
The plague! the plague! the plague!—
Oh, the wind Khamsin,
The scourge from the desert, blew in!

THE RIDE

We rose in the clear, cool dawning, and greeted
the eastern star;
"To saddle!" — our shout rang sharply out
by the huts of Kerf Hawàr.
The dervish slept by the wayside, the dog still
dozed by the door,
No *yashmaked* maid, with her water-jar, bent
low by the swift stream's shore.
The poplar leaves, as we mounted, turned white
in the veering wind,
And the icy peak of Hermon shone pyramidal
behind.

We had looked on the towers of Hebron, and
seen the sunlight wane
Over Zion's massive citadel, and Omar's holy
fane;
We had passed with pilgrim footsteps over
Judah's rocks and rills,

And seen the anemone-torches flare on the
Galilean hills.
But our eager hearts cried, "Onward! — be-
yond are the fairest skies;
Where rippling Barada silvers down, the bower
of the Prophet lies."

So we plunged through the tranquil twilight,
ere the sun rolled grandly up,
And brimmed the sky with its amber as Leba-
non wine a cup.
We dashed down the bare, brown *wadies*, where
echo cried from the crag;
There was never a hoof to linger, and never a
foot to lag;
We raced where the land lay level, and we
spurred it, black and bay,
Till the crimson bud of the morning flowered
full into dazzling day.

The dim, dark speck in the distance grew green
and broad and large,
And lo! a minaret's slender spear on the line
of its northern marge.
Then oh, what a cheer we lifted, and oh, how
we forward flew,

And oh, the balm of the greeting breeze that
out from the gardens blew!
And now we rode in the shadow of boughs
that were blossom-sweet,
While the gurgle of crystal waters rilled up
through the swooning heat.

Pink were the proud pomegranates, a rosy
cloud to the sight,
And the fluttering bloom of the orange was
white in the zenith light;
And sudden, or ever we dreamed it, did the
orchards give apart,
And there was the bowered city with the flood
of its orient heart;
There was the endless pageant that surged
through the arching gate;
There was the slim Bride's Minaret, and the
ancient "street called Straight."

And now that the ride was ended, there was
rest for man and beast;
For our trusty steeds there was shelter, and
grain for a goodly feast;
For us there were growing marvels, and a
wonder-wealth untold,

In the opulent glow of the daytime, in night
with its moon of gold.
For sherbet and song and roses, with a love-
smile flashed between,
Recur like the beat of a measure in the life of
a Damascene.

We will rise in dreams, belovëd, by the gleam
of the morning star,
And ride to the pearl of cities from the huts of
Kerf Hawàr.

THE SHÊKH ABDALLAH

What does the Shêkh Abdallah do
In the long, dull time of the Ramadan?
Why, he rises and says his prayers, and then
He sleeps till the prayer-hour comes again;
And thus through the length of the weary day
Does he sleep and pray, and sleep and pray.
Whenever the swart muezzin calls
From the crescent-guarded minaret walls,
Up he leaps and bows his turbaned brows
Toward Mecca, this valiant and holy man,
The Shêkh Abdallah—praise be to Allah!—
In the long, dull time of the Ramadan.

What does the Shêkh Abdallah do
In the long, dull time of the Ramadan?
Why, he fasts and fasts without reprieve,
From the blush of morn till the blush of eve.
Never so much as a sip takes he
Of the fragrant juice of the Yemen berry;
He shakes no fruit from the citron-tree,

Nor plucks the pomegranate, nor tastes the
cherry.
His sandal beads seem to tell of deeds
That were wrought by the hand of the holy
man,
The Shêkh Abdallah — praise be to Allah! —
In the long, dull time of the Ramadan.

What does the Shêkh Abdallah do
In the long, dull time of the Ramadan?
Why, he calls his servants, and just as soon
As in the copses the night-birds croon
A roasted kid is brought steaming in,
And then does the glorious feast begin;
Smyrna figs and nectarines fine,
Golden flasks of Lebanon wine,
Sherbet of rose and pistachios,
All are spread for the holy man,
The Shêkh Abdallah — praise be to Allah! —
In the long, dull time of the Ramadan.

What does the Shêkh Abdallah do
In the long, dull time of the Ramadan?
Why, when the cloying feast is o'er,
Dancers foot it along the floor;

Night-long to the sound of lute and viol
There is wine-mad mirth and the lilt of song,
And loving looks that brook no denial
From a radiant, rapturous throng.
" Morn calls to prayers, now away with cares ! "
He cries (this *faithful* and *holy* man !),
The Shêkh Abdallah —praise be to Allah !—
In the long, dull time of the Ramadan.

EASTER EVE AT KERAK-MOAB

THE fiery mid-March sun a moment hung
Above the bleak Judean wilderness;
Then darkness swept upon us, and 't was night.
The brazen day had stifled. On our eyes,
That throbbed and stung, the dusk fell like a
balm.
We lay and looked and listened. The warm
wind
Blew low and lutelike, and a fountain's fret
Made sweeter melody than all the streams
That gush from Nebo to far Sinai.
A strange-voiced bird among the thicket thorns
Sang to a star. The jackals loud resumed
Their weird nocturnal quarrels, and the laugh
Of some hill-strayed hyena broke across
The wild-dog's bickerings, — ironic, mad.
The palms that waved o'er squalid Jericho
Towered ghostly, and the Moab mountains
made
An inky line along the eastern sky.

Behind us bulky Quarantana gloomed,
And there a beacon, from a rock-cut cave,
Pricked the black night with its keen point of
fire.

Demetrius Domian, trusty dragoman,
Good friend and comrade, hale and handsome
Greek,
On elbow leaning, pointed one bronzed hand
Toward the vast, vague, and misty land that lay
Beyond the sacred Jordan. "There," he said,
A quaver breaking his deep-chested voice, —
"There, in wild Moab, Kerak-Moab lies."
Ofttimes before when day had spent its heat,
And in the wide tent doorway we reclined
On carpets Damascene, our guide had told
Strange tales adventurous, — of desert rides
Toward lonely Tadmor and old Bagdad shrines;
Of wanderings with the Meccan caravan
Where to be known a Christian was to die;
Of braving Druses in their Hauran haunts,
Where they kept guard o'er treasures of dead
kings
In cities overthrown. Such tales as these
Had 'livened many a quiet evening hour

After long pilgrimage. So when the Greek
Would fain dispel our homeward-turning
thoughts,
We gave him ready ear. This tale he told
In clear narration: —

"Nigh three years have seen
The olives ripen round Jerusalem
Since from St. Stephen's gateway I set forth
For Kerak-Moab with young Ibraim.
My cousin he, a comely youth, whom love
Had won with soft allurements. He would wed
A Kerak maid upon blest Easter Day,
And I must thither with him, — such his will,
Which I in no wise had desire to thwart;
For when his mother lay at brink of death,
(His father having long put off this life),
She bade me be a brother unto him,
And brother-like we were.

"Before us rode
Our servant, bearing on his sturdy beast
The needs for shelter on our lonely way,
And food therewith, and gifts to glad the bride.
By Kedrith's gloomy gorge, and Jericho,

And Jordan's ford, we journeyed; then our
path
Past Heshbon led us, and near Baal-Meon,
Where, records say, Elisha first drew breath.
The fifth day's sun was westering ere we saw
The antique gray of Kerak-Moab's towers,
And the all-crowning citadel.

"A warm,
Heart-moving welcome greeted us, and soon
Amid the kinsfolk of the bride to be
In merriment the jostling words went round.
'T was Easter Eve. The house wherein that
night
We were to shelter stood anear a breach
Within the wall that bulwarked round the town.
An ancient wall it was, Crusader-built,
And doubtless shattered by those Paynim
hordes
That northward surged from arid Araby,
Setting Mohammed's name o'er that of Christ;
And it was here the father of the bride
Had reared his goodly dwelling. Night was old
Before we left his roof to seek the door
That gracious kin had left unbarred for us.

Along the lanelike streets in silvery pools
The moonlight gleamed. From distant house-
tops bayed,
In broken iteration, Moslem dogs,
But 'twixt their baying all was desert-still.
'Why should we go within?' Ibraim said.
'Come, dear Demetrius, on this night of nights,
The last, perchance, that I shall pass with thee,
In this sweet air let us remain awhile,
And talk as brothers; for my life will soon
Be strangely changed, and though we oft may
meet,
Yet will there be another tongue to speak;
But now we are alone.'

"Arm linked in arm
We sought the breach, and spying in the wall
A nook where we could clamber, high above,
And wide o'erlooking all the moonlit scene,
We scrambled to it. There the hyssop grew,
And rugged seats invited to recline.
Then, while he told me his fond tale of love
Over again for quite the hundredth time,
I mused upon the future, vacant-eyed,
Beholding nothing. When his happy speech

Had run its course, and silence jarred me back
To ambient things, my conscious vision caught
A shadowy glimpse of one swift-skulking form,
From fragment unto fragment of prone wall
In phantom quiet flitting. While I gazed,
Another and another followed fast,
Till, as I gripped Ibraim's arm, a score
In sudden sight from black concealment rose,
And forward gliding noiselessly, below
Our lofty cranny paused. Anxious, alert,
We listened breathlessly, and then we heard —
Just God! but how we started when we heard,
And horror-mute stared in each other's eyes,
That moment haggard grown!

"Then down we slipped,
And in the shadow by the breach's edge
Where dropped the wall nigh two men's height
away
To sloping ground, with faces set, and hands
Fast clutching weapon hilts, we stood in wait.
We dared not leave the breach. The robber
band,
Once in the town, would spread through sinu-
ous lanes

And sow destruction ; and the first to fall
Beneath their ruthless power might be the ones
To whom by love-ties was Ibraim bound.
We felt that here their onset we must face,
And with that onset lift our cry for aid.
Their parley ceased. A moment, and we saw
Two stealthy forms rise, black against the moon,
Propped by their comrades on the ground
below.
Then pealed our wildest shout, and on the
twain
We flung ourselves so madly they were hurled
Sheer backward on the heads below. A space
The band retreated, but when they divined
That we alone stood guard, while still our cries
Vibrated down the corridors of night,
In one close mass they rushed upon the breach,
Like some huge wave that, when the seas are
fierce,
Rolls on the ruined battlements of Tyre,
Clutches their base, and reaches clinging arms,
To clasp the loftiest stone.

"Then from its sheath,
Where like a coilëd serpent round my waist

Slept my curved blade of keen Damascus steel,
I whipped it forth, as drew Ibraim his.
A deadly circle did we flash in air,
And on that human wave fell vengefully.
Twice, thrice, we smote, and while, unharmed,
I clove
A fourth black-turbaned crown, I saw two
fiends
Leap at Ibraim. As he slew the first
The other seized him in his demon grasp,
And, like one frenzied, sprang through middle
space
Upon the writhing throng.

"Along the street
The tardy rescuers surged. I cried them on ;
But when they came, the wily Bedouin foe
Had sought the shielding shadow of the night.

"I raised Ibraim's head : his heavy lids
Fluttered a moment, and around his mouth
A sad smile hovered, as he breathed my name
And that of his belovëd. Death was bride
Of brave Ibraim on that Easter Eve."

Demetrius paused, and leaned upon his palm.
A sudden wind tore at the tent. Above,
Black clouds had gulfed the stars. A bodeful
moan
Grew momently amid the dark defiles;
The livid lightning rent the breast of night,
Then burst the brooding storm. But lo! at
dawn
Peace smiled upon the plain of Jericho,
And all the line of Moab mountains lay
Golden and glad beneath the risen sun.

THE MOSQUE OF THE SULTAN HASSAN

By Arabian tomes we are told
He was just, as a ruler and man, —
The Caliph of Cairo the old,
The Sultan Hassan.

One day did he hear of the fame
Of a builder, and straightway he said:
"I will build me a mosque that my name
May outlive me when dead."

So he summoned this man to his throne
And issued his royal decree:
"Uprear me a temple of stone
For the years that shall be;

"Uprear me a wonderful shrine
Where 'the faithful' of Allah may bow;
And glorious meed shall be thine;
Here record I the vow."

Then the heart of the builder was light
  As was ever the heart of a man;
And he toiled through the gloom of the night,
  And he wrought him a plan, —

A plan of a mosque that should bind
  His name with the name of his lord.
So the slaves brought the marble they mined,
  And they wrought in accord,

Till the mosque as by magic upsprang
  In its symmetry peerless and grand;
And the praise and the fame of it rang
  Through the length of the land.

But the name of the builder was cried
  Till the Caliph grew wroth at the sound;
"Am I naught?" he would mutter in pride;
  "Am I less than a hound;

"And this chiefest of upstarts so great
  He eclipses the light of my throne?"
Thus the seeds of a pitiless hate
  In his bosom were sown.

Now the mosque was complete. Without peer
Was the portal majestic and tall;
The minarets tapering sheer
From the sweep of the wall.

In the court was a fountain that flowed,
And its pillars were cunningly scrolled;
And the *mambar* was marble that glowed
With mosaics of gold.

"Call the builder!" said Sultan Hassan;
They ran at the word of their lord;
"My servant," he thought, as they ran,
"Now shall reap his reward."

At the steps of the throne knelt the one
Who had served like a slave at the soil;
Said the Caliph, "Thy task-work is done,
Here is meed for thy toil;

"Stretch thy hands! I would pay thee full well."
The builder obeyed, in his trust;
Then a scimitar flashed, and they fell
Reeking red in the dust.

"No more," said the Caliph revered,
"I would have thee to build. I decree
It is honor enough, by my beard,
To have builded for me!"

*By Arabian tomes we are told
He was just, as a ruler and man, —
The Caliph of Cairo the old,
The Sultan Hassan.*

MELIK THE BLACK

WHERE has the Princess gone —
  The Princess Parizade?
The dazzling glow of the Orient dawn
  Floods down through the garden glade.
She is not in the room where the air is sweet
  With the scent of the attared rose,
And the tinkle of silver-sandaled feet
  Like a brook o'er the marble flows;
She is not in the mosque nor the dim kiosk,
  She is not in the almond-close.

Melik the black stands mute
  By the harem's outer door;
Does he dream of the sound of the Sennar flute,
  And the warm Nile nights of yore?
Does he muse on the happy, bondless days
  By the desert fountains cool,
When he rode his barb o'er the trackless ways,
  Ere he came to be the tool

Of the loves and hates in the palace gates
  Of the treacherous Istamboul?

His thoughts are not afar
  In the wide, free Southern land;
He sees, as he saw 'neath the paling star,
  A tiny print in the sand.
There hangs the slender ladder yet
  Where the daring flight was made;
On the water-stair the ooze and wet
  Betray where the boat was stayed;
She has fled o'er the main from her gilded
    chain —
  The Princess Parizade.

And shall he bide to face
  His master's merciless wrath?
Woe on the soul that waits for grace
  In a maddened tyrant's path!
But list! — o'er the court's mosaic floor
  Creeps one with a panther tread,
Behind the form at the harem door,
  With the mournful, low-drooped head.
A dagger bright in the morning light! —
  And Melik the black lies dead.

IN THE HARARA

UNCUMBERED and supine I lie,
An azure dome my mimic sky;
Smooth, shining walls around I see,
As white as new-cut ivory,
Save where one sinuous purple line
Creeps up the marble like a vine.
The crystal stream that o'er me runs
Has felt the glow of Syrian suns,
And swift through all my being flows,
Not the keen chill of Hermon snows,
But such a latent fire as sleeps
Within the grape on Lebanon steeps.

Now comes my genie of the ring
A lighted narghileh to bring;
Against my longing lips I set
Its deftly polished tube of jet.
The quiet water in the bowl
Seems suddenly to own a soul;

The bubbles form, and swell, and break,
And incoherent murmurs make,
While visions fair before my eyes
In upward-curling clouds arise ;
I catch the soothing scent divine
Of Latakia rich and fine.

Oh, is it strange I should forget
The world of turmoil and of fret ;
For one sweet hour should play no part,
But be a Syrian to the heart !
Clasp idleness unto my breast,
And drain the very dregs of rest ;
Know all the joy that Haroun knew,
And feel the power of Timur too !
But dreams have end, and once again
I rouse me to life's real domain,
To hold forevermore in fee
The Orient's charm and mystery.

A NILE NIGHT.

THE wind has died ; to-day we sail no more
  O'er river reaches widening bright or wan ;
Languid we lie beside the reedy shore,
  And night draws darkly on.

In no wise strange or pagan would it seem
  To Pasht or Isis now to bend the knee,
There broods about us, in day's paling beam,
  Such vast antiquity.

Yonder a sacred ibis, grave as faith,
  Stands like a statue by the river brink ;
And mark ! is that a Libyan lion's wraith
  Come to the stream to drink ?

A wandering minstrel pipes a plaintive strain,
  Then slowly, sadly, lets the music swoon ;
While, like a lovely lotus, once again
  Flowers the Egyptian moon.

And so to rest, and visions weirdly clear
Of priests, of kings, of gods with hoof and horn,
To rouse at last from dreams wherein we hear
Great Memnon greet the morn.

A REED.

WHOSO shall blow this slender reed,
On swift aërial wings will speed,
And 'neath the lofty palm-boughs stand
Where Nilus lips the Libyan sand.

There was it cut and shaped, and still
Delicious tremors through it thrill, —
Low and mysterious murmurings drawn
From waves on some mid-Afric dawn.

Within its hollow heart there lies
This mystery of mysteries ;
Then blow and test the trancëd spell,
Morn-wrought in Music's crucible !

THE BRONZE CHRIST.

THE monarch looked out from his throne
Where the Bosphorus blends with the Horn,
And he saw how at evening and morn
The people would prayerfully bow
To figures of bronze and of stone ;
And he cried, as he smote on his brow,
"They worship the image alone ;
Forgot is the Godhead behind.
Their prayers are but words on the wind
That hither and thither are blown."

Then an edict went forth from the south
To the north of the empire afar,
And a herald with clamorous mouth
Proclaimed it in hamlet and town,
Till the folk as by rumors of war
Were stirred, or by famine and drouth,
For from niche and from altar and shrine
The Christ and the Virgin divine
Must be cast desecratingly down.

So rage slumbered hot in the heart
In Constantine's city, the old ;
And murmurs waxed loud in the mart,
And the tongues of the people grew bold.
But the monarch was firm ; and the more,
When he heard of the stir in the state,
Was his spirit alert and elate,
And naught in his rashness sufficed
But to cry to the guard at the door,
"Thou knowest the image of Christ
Surmounting the palace's gate ;
Go thou, take thy weapon and smite,
In the emperor's name and the right ! "

The guardsman was pallid with fear,
For he knew how the Christ was adored,
But he only could bow and obey,
Passing forth on his perilous way
With his hand gripping tight on his sword.
By the gate was a woman in prayer,
Who, when she beheld his intent,
Cried loud to the heralding air,
Till there gathered around her a score.
There were crones in decrepitude bent,
And mothers, and maids who were fair,
To beg and beseech and implore.

But he gave little heed to their cries,
For he dreaded the emperor's ire;
He saw not the light in their eyes,
The baleful and dangerous fire.
The ladder was scaled, and his hand
Uplifted the merciless brand;
A glimmer of steel and a blow,
And the image fell clanging below
In the midst of the sorrowful band.

In a moment their grief was forgot,
And a frenzy possessed them instead.
Afar from the doom-fated spot
Would the terrified guardsman have fled;
But they seized him in madness, and tore
His limbs in their maniac might,
And dabbled their hands in his gore,
And shouted with awful delight
That Christ was avenged evermore.

A tale of the shadowy past
Obscured by the mists of the years,
Where, down all the distance, one hears
Fanatical echoes of strife.

Oh, why, from the first to the last,
Should His name, that the spirit reveres,
Be blent with the clashing of spears
Where frenzy and slaughter are rife !

Love, love was the creed that He taught,
And peace, perfect peace, everywhere ;
The past that is dead is as naught,
The present and future are fair.
Could we but see over the tomb
The flowers of Christ's tenderness bloom,
Grand, grand were the ages to come,
For the voices of strife would be dumb !

MIRAGE

"Behold, behold the palms!" we cried;
  Our lips were parched as though by fire;
Forward we spurred with swinging stride,
  In madness of desire.

"There will be water cool!" we said,
  "And shade to shield from blazing heat;
What bliss to bathe the burning head,
  And oh, the rest, how sweet!"

But suddenly — the palms were gone!
  A scorching breeze our swart brows fanned;
Before us still stretched on and on
  A blinding waste of sand.

THE PRAYER

The slender leaves of the acacia-trees
Hung parched and quivering in the desert breeze.

Straight westward, as a starving rook might fly,
One pyramid's dark apex cut the sky;

While sharp against the sapphire east were set
Resplendent dome and soaring minaret.

Beside the way, upon his prayer-mat prone,
A turbaned suppliant made his plaint alone.

The hot sun smote upon his humbled head;
"*Allah, have pity!*" — this was all he said.

His faltering tongue forgot the accustomed art,
And laid his unvoiced grief on Allah's heart.

IN GILEAD

THIS is the land of Gilead, but where is the
fabled balm,
Unless it lie in the placid sky, in the sapphire
leagues of calm?
Here grows no balsam-bearing bough, no
fruitage-yielding palm.

The dark-browed sons of the desert, they tend
the flocks that feed
On the hillside slopes where the myrtle gleams,
and the mustard wings its seed,
And they pluck the reed by the Jabbok's
marge and pipe while the waters speed.

In spring is the oleander fair with a faint pink
flush of bloom;
The jackal makes his home with kings in the
deepest rock-cut tomb,
And the fierce hyena's cry is weird in the mid-
night's purple gloom.

And thou, O Ramoth-Gilead, how lies thy splendor low!
Though still does Jedur's fountain gush in never-failing flow,
And purl through sweet pomegranate-bowers and olive groves below.

Within thy walls, O Jerash, still stands thy mighty gate
That oft saw Roman legions pass in gilded pomp of state;
Now they are gone, and gone thy power, yet thou in death art great.

Look down, look down, from Gilead! There Jordan winds its way,
And silvery bright the Dead Sea sleeps beneath the tropic day;
Look up, look up, where Nebo stands, a bulwark vast and gray!
Yet who would bide in Gilead, though cloudless be her skies,
Though stair on stair through crystal air her massive mountains rise?
Beneath the glorious western star *our* blessëd Gilead lies!

THE PALM OF JENIN

How fair has been the bland bright day! how fair
The emerald hill-sweep, and the blue of air
Pulsating o'er the earth; the long sweet hours
Enlinked with rainbow chains of honeyed flowers;
Flowers on the slopes, the plains, flowers everywhere,
Anemone, primrose, and poppy-bowers!
Was ever any day before so fair?

And now that all the west is one warm line,
The ruby hue of lip-enthralling wine,
And now that flocks wend fold-ward, bleating low,
And brown-limbed pipers follow, footing slow,
Will we upon the velvet sod recline,

And let across our brows the cool breeze blow,
And turn our faces toward the red sky-line.

Lo! in the sunset's heart one patriarch palm,
A silhouette upon the evening calm,
Catches the wandering eye that fain would rest
Upon the changing wonders of the west;
And while a bird uplifts a twilight psalm
Above his mate in her leaf-hidden nest,
We watch the black-etched frondage of the palm.

Companionless and solitary now,
It once had fellows straight of trunk and bough,
And there were gardens glad with bloom around
Where fountains tossed their silver coin of sound;
Then came the desert's son with turbaned brow
And cast a blight upon the fertile ground.
Alas! one palm-tree only greets us now.

And yet this palm's firm bole says, "I endure!
I wait the rising day that dawneth sure,
  The day when Islam's might shall be o'er-
    thrown,
  And all its prowess lie as shattered stone;
Then will my lovely land again be pure,
  My hills again with teeming harvests groan;
For such a glorious day do I endure."

Would that the coming morn, O stately tree,
Such dear deliverance might bring to thee!
  But still the darkness deepens. We behold
  The new moon's scimitar of jealous gold.
The Crescent reigns; the fathomless To-be
  Thy fate within its sealëd heart doth hold,
And Time alone can speak, O noble tree!

SPRING IN GALILEE

Once more the yearly miracle has made
The patient earth rejoice.
Came it when night's purpureal shade
Hid heaven's canopy, the loving voice
That bade the green grass break
Its shining sheath and shake
Its myriad spears? that bade the flowering brush
With bloomy ardors flush?
That spoke with such a thrill,
The blossom-beacons flamed from hill to hill?

Man heard it not, but listening nature heard
The swift-reviving word;
Heard, and with one glad leap
Sprang from forgetful sleep,
Till now an emerald, undulating main
Is wide Esdraelon's plain,
Whereon, while bland winds blow,
The clumsy camel-craft drift to and fro.

And orchard-girdled Nazareth once more
Kindles at heart with throbs of young desire;
Here are the turbaned merchants come from
        Tyre
And ancient Acre, with their precious store.
And through the bright bazaars,
With heavy-lidded eyes like drowsing stars,
A dark-robed, dusky desert-minstrel goes,
Thrumming upon his single-stringëd lyre,
And lilting songs that swell to joyful close.

And Nazareth's daughters, radiantly fair,
With midnight woven in their braided hair,
And on their cheeks the rose and olive blent,
And in their eyes a prisoned Orient,
Come, with their jars a-poise
On queenly heads, down to the Virgin's Well;
And there their griefs and joys
In mellow monotone they tell,
Bending in graceful languor o'er the pool
That mirrors them in waters clear and cool.

Could we but roll
The crowding centuries backward like a scroll,
These paths would know His feet,

And hear His kindly voice so calm and sweet.
He must have loved the spring, —
The resurrection, the re-bourgeoning,
The quickened pulse in nature's every vein,
The skyward-mounting strain.
Fairer to us is all this fairness now,
That He once trod
Where swaying poppies burn above the sod,
And stood on yonder mountain's hallowed brow.

Here is the spring-time fraught
With larger meanings than on other earth;
A deeper sense of a diviner birth,
For all humanity, is caught;
And broader life we see
When spring illumes the slopes of Galilee.

A SONNET OF SONNETS

I

THE NILE

NURSE of old Egypt, year on circling year,
When parched and fevered by the heat she lies
Beneath a dazzling arch of rainless skies,
And e'en the green acacia buds grow sere,
How dost thou brim a cup supremely dear
And hold it to her lips, until her sighs
Have ceased, and all before her ancient eyes
Is fair as erst it was, or far or near!

Whence hast thou this fine potion? Is it drawn
From cavernous founts that never see the dawn
Beyond swart Nubia's furthermost confines?
So potent yet mysterious it seems,
Its source might be within a heaven of dreams
Upon whose peaks no earthly sunbeam shines.

II

AN ARAB BOY

THIS brown-skinned boy whose hair in heavy curl
About his low and wide-set forehead falls,
And who "*baksheesh*" vociferously calls,
Whose parted lips reveal a flash of pearl,
Is come of those who in the rush and swirl
Of battle shout, at frenzied intervals,
"*Allah il Allah*," till the sky's blue walls
Above them seem to madly reel and whirl.

Ah! what a lustre fires his handsome eye!
Already gleams the fate-implanted spark
One day may kindle to a lurid glow:
His mouth is set for some barbaric cry,
His lithe frame quivers wrathfully, and mark!
His hand is clenched for a fanatic blow.

III

AN EGYPTIAN NIGHT

THE tropic night has reached its splendid noon ;
  What magic has bewitched the wayward
      breeze
  In winter's heart to scatter balms like these,
And wake the birds to ecstasies of tune ?
No dream is this of occidental June,
  For mark yon minaret that soars the seas
  Of silver air, and trace the soft degrees
Of shade beneath the palms that greet the
      moon.

Like undulating serpent-coils unrolled,
The Nile sends down its tide of tawny gold ;
  While with impassive, never-drowsing lids,
And scarred, yet smiling, unbetraying lips,
Holding their speech forever in eclipse,
  The dark Sphinx crouches by the pyramids.

IV

A HEAD OF ISIS

WHAT suppliant thought thee sacred long ago,
  O faultless, chilly lips of sculptured stone,
  Making before thee tearful plaint and moan,
Beseeching thee to ease her bitter woe?
Was love unkind? — alas! we may not know.
  Above her tomb the sands are piled and blown;
  And thou, — thou hast no longer shrine, nor throne,
Nor worshipers before thee bending low.

Thou art a wraith of deity downcast;
  She that besought thee is forgotten dust,
    But Love, or kind or cruel, still lives on:
Shall *we* leave aught to the engulfing past
  Save empty tombs disfigured by grim rust,
    Or lifeless masks for men to gaze upon?

V

THE PALMS

Above the sand-heaped grave where Memphis lies
Impassive and disconsolate they tower;
The peerless skies above them never lower,
The desert winds intone their requiem sighs;
As decade after fleeting decade dies,
They brood upon the past, — its mighty power;
To-day is naught; their life is but a dower
Of vain regrets, — of haunting memories.

At dusk they change. By Titan hands is reared
Out of the sable quarries of the night
A phantom city, silent, sombre, lone;
Lo! in their stead loom temples vast and weird,
Bearded colossi rising height on height
Around great Rameses and his spectral throne.

VI

SAKARA[1]

A BLAZING reach of undulating sand;
No cooling shade, no breeze save one that blows
O'er leagues of desert, burning in repose;
A cloudless sky by fiery arches spanned;
One crumbling pyramid, grim, gray, and grand,
Holding within its heart the tombëd woes
Of dateless centuries, whose pangs and throes
Are vaguer than the shapes of shadow-land.

Could but the serried ages backward sweep,
The desolating desert take its own,
And some bright-gloried Memphian morning dawn,
Yet should we see, where now the sand lies deep,
Death regnant on his immemorial throne,
With silence round him like a mantle drawn.

[1] Sakara, — the necropolis of Memphis.

VII

A SHELL

WHAT liquid music this white whorl hath heard,
And what tempestuous, drowning symphonies,
Forever hearkening at the changeful sea's
Great lips to catch the faintest whispered word!
Still is the sense of sound within it stirred; —
Is it the echo of the flute-toned breeze,
The siren's song, the waves' wild melodies,
Or none of these, — or all divinely blurred?

Lend thou attentive ear! This vocal shell
Hath listed Egypt's heart-throbs, and the sound
Of Nile's mysterious voice whose murmur links
The known and the unknown that hath no bound;
Perchance, — who knows? — if thou but heedest well,
Thou mayest learn the secret of the Sphinx!

VIII

MEMNON

WHY dost thou hail with songful lips no more
The glorious sunrise?—Why is Memnon mute,
Whose voice was tuned as is the silvery flute
When Thebes sat queenly by the Nile's low shore?
The chained slaves sweat no longer at the oar,
No longer shrines are raised to man and brute,
Yet dawn by dawn the sun thou didst salute
Gives thee the greeting that it gave of yore.

What nameless spell is on thee? Dost thou wait
(Hoping and yearning through the years forlorn)
The old-time splendor and the regal state,
The glory and the power of empire shorn?
Oh, break the silence deep, defying fate,
And cry again melodious to the morn!

IX

THE OASIS

DOES sight deceive? are yonder palms outlined
  Against the lurid sky a desert dream?
  How often has a fair, elusive gleam
Of foliage lured us! Now the freshening wind
Fans their slim fronds, and shadows cool and kind
  Await before. The camels scent the stream
  Of welcome water. Soon the day-orb's beam
Our hot and aching eyes no more will blind.

How soft the greensward is! and oh, what bliss
To feel upon our lips the water's kiss!
  And hark! as clear as Hafiz heard in Pharz,
The nightingale salutes the day's calm close,
The while we seek the guerdon of repose,
  Our tent the night, our lights the watchful stars.

X

A DERVISH

LIKE Joseph's coat his tattered raiment shows
A rainbow blending of its countless hues;
The desert dust has stained his pilgrim shoes,
His frame is gaunt, yet on and on he goes.
Few are the hours his weary limbs repose,
Few are the drops that wet his earthen cruse;
The path is long, the sharp flints cut and bruise,
And yet at heart a dreamful rest he knows.

His visions are of calm celestial days,
Of peaceful groves of palm beyond the skies;
Forever shine before his ardent eyes
The fountained heavenly courts through golden haze:
He deems the more he bears on mortal ways
The greater his reward in Paradise.

XI

BUBASTIS

HERE were majestic temples reared of yore,
  Vast marble halls and columned porticos;
  Here maidens garlanded the sacred rose,
And throngs passed singing by the river shore.
Hither long barques pipe-playing pilgrims bore,
  And wine ran bright until the dim night's close;
  Here men sought solace for all mortal woes, —
The goddess held divine forevermore.

Long stilled is now each priest's prophetic tongue,
  Sekhet has fallen from her empire grand,
    In formless heaps of dust her shrines are traced;
  Relentlessly sweeps in the shrouding sand,
And where the sound of choiring voices rung,
    The jackals howl forlornly o'er the waste.

XII

AT HELIOPOLIS

A PATIENT ox plods round a water-wheel;
A fervent Moslem breathes his noonday vows;
In clover fields beneath the tamarisk boughs
The heavy-lidded, clumsy camels kneel.
The whirling swallows sound their plaintive peal;
Repulsive beggars by the roadside drowse;
One hoary obelisk lifts its scarrëd brows
Whereon of old a monarch set his seal.

Of all the stately monoliths that here
Once tapered skyward, this slim shaft and gray
Alone remains, defying hoary time.
Beyond cold seas, in many an alien clime,
Its comrades mark the birth and death of day,
And exiled, mourn the bland Egyptian year.

XIII

THE MUEZZIN

It is the swift, sweet, Orient sunset hour;
  And o'er the city, as the daylight dies,
  In melancholy monotone one cries
An exhortation from a tall mosque tower.
The almond-tree is whitening into flower,
  A vernal gladness on the garden lies;
  There is a softness in the wind that sighs
Amid the branches of the orange-bower.

Two lovers whisper in the perfumed air;
  A bird's clear melody is heard above;
He tells the story to his feathered fair
  The happy twain below are dreaming of.
That distant call proclaims the hour of prayer;
  Their murmured vows proclaim the hour of
    love.

XIV

THE SPHINX

COUCHANT upon the illimitable sand,
Like some huge Libyan lion, human-faced,
The solemn march of centuries thou hast traced
With brooding eyes that seem to understand
The secrets of the ages, — whose the hand
That rolls the stars along the ethereal waste,
And for what purpose suffering man is placed
Upon this orb, to be or blessed or banned.

In elder years did suppliants bend the knee
Before thine awful presence reverently,
Beseeching answer with adoring breath;
Yet wert thou mute, as thou wilt ever be,
Enigma, like our mortal destiny,
Inscrutable as is the face of death.

A DAMASCUS BLADE

THIS crescent-shaped and flexile blade,
With time-dulled, tawny gold inlaid,
'Neath skies that knew the Eastern star
Was found within an old bazaar.
I mind me well, how, passing by,
We caught the merchant's gleaming eye,
Where in his dim recess he sat
Upon his precious Persian mat.
Urbane he was and grave of mien,
This patriarchal Damascene;
He lured us to his small divan,
A serving-boy for coffee ran,
And, while we sipped, he laid before
Our widening eyes his wondrous store.

There from worn sheaths, once bright with gilt,
We saw protrude the jeweled hilt;
There ivory from Bengal brought
With Saracenic art was wrought;
And there keen steel we looked upon

That like moon-burnished water shone.
But most of all on me laid hold
This blade, with letters strangely scrolled, —
Some curious Koran text, no doubt,
Bidding the warrior's heart be stout, —
And, when we took our way afar,
I bore it from the old bazaar.

He had a deadly-supple wrist
Who wielded it of yore, I wist;
And oft, mayhap, in goodly stead,
He flashed it o'er his turbaned head,
When some Crusader, huge and grim,
In the thick press confronted him.
Perchance his zealous soul now roves
In peaceful paradisial groves;
His blade — I wonder does he know? —
Is nothing but a curio!
Ah! what a fate its fate has been, —
The blade that cleft for Saladin!

THE GOLDEN STREAM

CHRYSORRHOAS

Why thy mellow name we know not,
  Given by the Greeks of old,
For the ancient records show not
  If thy sands were bright with gold.

Clear thou art: no nectar clearer
  E'er a pilgrim's praises won;
And the Prophet held thee dearer
  Than the wine of Lebanon.

Men with solemn rites adored thee
  Where thou sprang'st, at crystal birth,
Strong as though a god had poured thee
  From the urns of under-earth.

Fairer gardens there were never
  Gazed upon by Shêkh or Shah,

Than where thou dost rill forever
  Through the meads of Bessima.

There the apricot blooms brightly,
  And the fig-tree never fails;
And within the poplars nightly
  Sing the Eastern nightingales.

There with Love in calm seclusion,
  What were life but bliss supreme! —
All its trials but illusion,
  All its tumult but a dream!

Golden river, — stream elysian,
  With thy love-enchanted shore,
Through my memory, like a vision,
  Flow thou on forevermore!

A KORAN

MOROCCO-BOUND, before me lies
A curious volume that I prize;
Upon the final page of it,
In eastern character, is writ
The name of him who found therein
A shield against the shafts of sin.
With long and arduous toil I spell
Slow, syllable by syllable:
"Abdul Hafiz," — the name I see, —
"Hegira-year nine eighty-three."

My ardent fancy pictures him
Within a court-yard cool and dim;
Around him, grouped with studious air,
Are many a tiny turbaned pair
Who con aloud their tasks in low,
Soft voices while the dull hours go,
Or catch from off his bearded lip
The hoarded wisdom he lets slip,

His dark eye often resting on
The very book I gaze upon.

And though I may not read its page
As did the ancient Moslem sage,
Yet hath the Orient tome for me
More charm than mere antiquity.
It seems to widely backward throw
The barrier doors of long ago;
And centuried corridors along
I hear the lute-like sound of song;
What touched a chord in Hafiz' heart
Must have of good some golden part!

THE CALIPH'S PILLAR

In the lotus-land, ere the crescent's splendor
   Had waned 'neath the arch of the rainless
      skies,
A Caliph ruled as the faith's defender,
   Brave, benignant, and grave, and wise.

To him came one who outcried, "O Master,
   I have reared a mosque where the highways
      meet,
And the pillared court lacks one pilaster,
   And so is closed to the pilgrim's feet.

"Oh, hearken thou to my prayer in pity!
   In the name of Allah give gracious aid!
Let a pillar, borne from the holy city,
   Fill the empty arch of the colonnade."

Then the Caliph said, "Thou hast wisely
      spoken,

From the Prophet's home shall the column
be,
And I, in search of the sacred token,
Will journey to Mecca, beyond the sea."

So his patient way o'er the wastes he wended,
Till he reached the place of the Prophet's
birth,
And there in worship his brow he bended
At the holiest shrine of the Moslem earth.

And when he had bathed at the healing foun-
tain,
And humbly bowed at the blessëd shrine,
And when he had knelt on the hallowed moun-
tain,
He sought a shaft from a marble mine.

He found one flawless as alabaster,
That gleamed in the glow of the Arab sun,
And he cried aloud to the fair pilaster,
"The shining goal of my search is won!

"Arise, O column, arise, O column!" —
Thus twice he called, but he called in vain;

Then he raised his lash, and in accents solemn,
As he smote the marble, he cried again:

"In the name of Allah thy bondage sunder,
And swift to the land of the Nile take flight!"
And lo! in the eyes of the throng this wonder, —
The smitten column was lost to sight.

And when to his mosque went the builder faring
In Egypt far, at the next day's verge,
He found the beautiful pillar bearing
The writhing mark of the Caliph's scourge.

The years are waves on the tide of ages;
Builder and Caliph alike are clay;
And empty names on the past's gray pages
Are all they seem to the world to-day.

But the mosque still stands with its smitten pillar,
And men still press through its arching gate,
To kneel in prayer, as the air grows stiller,
And murmur, "*Allah alone is great!*"

SHERBET

F. D. S.

FRIEND, ere the golden hours decline,
Enlink your loving arm with mine,
And let me lead your willing feet
Through maze on maze of winding street,
To where, beyond the gateway, lies
A bowery garden-paradise.
Each strident noise that grates or jars
We 'll leave within the packed bazaars;
For us the springing fount will show
The blending colors of its bow;
For us the poplars will display
Their changing silvery green and gray;
And neither voice nor lute will tire
Till stars the dreams of night inspire.

And while in idleness we drowse
Beneath the bloom-sweet citron boughs,
One, sandaled as with sleep, will bear
A draught to lay the wraith of care.

The rare Damascus rose's wine
Will lend to it a flavor fine,
And tides of crimson will impart
As rich as dye the blossom's heart.
Clear ice the brimming cup will cool,
Cut from some flawless mountain pool
On Hermon's massive shoulder, far
Above the huts of Kerf Hawàr;
And oh, what fancies as we drink
Will greet us at the beaker's brink!

Before our eyes will gleam and glance
The woven threads of old romance, —
Those fabrics fair that never fade,
Spun by the brave Scheherezade.
And we will list the trancëd tales
Of plaintive Shiraz nightingales,
Bemoaning love around the tomb
Where Hafiz sleeps in scented gloom.
His exile will Firdausi tell,
And Sadi weave his blossom-spell,
While one will chant in liquid line
His rapturous praises of the vine, —
Omar, whose fame the years prolong,
The zenith-star of Persian song.

No vintage-draught soe'er, compressed
From the broad bosom of the West,
Can yield the keen delight of this
Enthralling, roseate cup of bliss.
Then come, O friend ; quaff deep with me !
And Poesy our pledge shall be.

THE MINSTREL

He played on the single string
  Of a strange lute warped and old,
And sang and sang till the gray walls rang
  To the ditty weird he trolled.
Sweet was the languid air,
  The sun was hot and high,
And ruby-red the pomegranates spread
  Their bloom to the Syrian sky.

A turban green he wore,
  And a flowing robe of white:
With a rhythmic grace he moved, and his face
  Was black as the Nubian night.
Why had he strayed from the clime
  Where the scorching siroc blows,
To sing in the bowers of the citron flowers
  And the red Damascus rose?

I can but think he was one
  Of that dusky, mythic band

Who weave dark spells in the fountained dells
  Of the swart Arabian land;
A genie, slave of a ring,
  A roamer of earth and air,
At the will of some young Aladdin come
  To snare with a fatal snare.

His visage haunts me still,
  Haunts in the height of noon,
And again upfloats in wild low notes
  His mystic Arabic croon;
It lures me there once more
  Where the silvery Pharpar flows,
And I stray in the bowers of the citron flowers
  And the red Damascus rose!

A PRAYER CARPET

I KNOW not when in Daghestan
He lived, the skillful artisan,
Who wove in some mysterious way
This fabric where the colors play
Across the woof in rainbow chase,
Or meet and link and interlace.

Nor do I know what suppliant knees
Once pressed these yielding symmetries,
The while the turbaned brow was turned
Toward Mecca, and the soul that yearned,
Borne by the rapt muezzin cry,
Soared, bird-like, up the tranquil sky.

But this I know, — foot ne'er shall press
Its worship-hallowed loveliness,
For still about it dumbly clings
A subtle sense of holy things,
And woven in the meshes there
Are strands of vow and shreds of prayer.

With kindling morning beams the sun
Its blended colors shines upon;
The mosque domes catch the rays, and lo!
In loitering lines the camels go.
A fountain flings a silver jet;
A palm-tree cuts a silhouette.

But when night lids the eye of day,
And sunset glories fade away,
My fancy shapes a fervent man
From shadows on the Daghestan.
Thus, in its compass small, I see
The Orient in epitome.

THE SUN AND THE NEW MOON

In all its majesty of light revealed,
The vision-dazzling sun is Allah's shield;
While slender, keen, unmarred by flaw or scar,
The fair new moon is Allah's scimitar.

HADETH THE MARONITE

On the breeze-kissed mountain brow,
  On the brow of Lebanon,
Girt by the vine and bough,
  It looks toward the western sun;
It looks toward the sun, and the sea
  Blue below and afar,
On the olive groves and mulberry,
  Gray old Der-el-Kamar.

The well-tilled terraces reach
  The fronting slopes adown;
In spring the pink of the peach
  Bourgeons in orchards brown;
And the Eastern nightingale
  Beneath in the covert calls,
Where the curve of the crescent vale
  Sweeps round the battled walls.

In the troubled years agone,
  A tawny, turbaned band,

In the gray of the early dawn,
  Rode up through the mountain land;
Rode up through the vineyards fair
  While faded the morning star,
Till rose in the brightening air
  The walls of Der-el-Kamar.

The guard grew pale at the gate,
  But he bade them halt, nor pass;
They charged like a bolt of fate,
  And shivered the bar like glass.
Through the wakening streets they ran,
  In the glow of the new-born day;
They spared nor maid nor man
  In their frenzied thirst to slay.

To them 't was a holy strife,
  A boon in the Prophet's eyes;
An unarmed Christian's life
  Was a sacred sacrifice.
The skies caught up the wail,
  Blood ran like wine from a cruse;
Never an arm could avail
  Against the wrath of the Druse.

But Hadeth thought of his bride,
  And his mother, gray with years,
And he cast despair aside,
  And laughed to scorn his fears.
" Yet there is time," he said,
  " Ere the last defender fall,
To baffle the foeman dread
  By the break in the valley wall."

He gathered the old and young;
  Their feet seemed shod with the wind;
(But a furious shout out-rung
  From the demon horde behind.)
The break in the wall they reach;
  Who will shelter their flight?
See! he stands in the breach,
  Hadeth the Maronite.

Boldly he fronts them there, —
  The swarthy, surging foe;
His scimitar gleams in air
  Like the arc of an iris-bow.
Mad is their charge, but vain,
  For firmly he breasts the shock,
And stems the human main
  Like a battlement of rock.

Alas, for earthly power
  That hero-hearts should fall!
That wrong should rule the hour,
  And right be pressed to the wall!
Yet not till the weak who fled
  Were safe in the mountains far,
Did Hadeth the brave lie dead
  By the breach at Der-el-Kamar.

But none shall slay his name,
  This son of Der-el-Kamar;
Set in the sky of fame,
  Burns it a steadfast star.
While the seasons wheel around,
  And darkness follows the light,
Still shall his praise resound, —
  Hadeth the Maronite.

MUSTAPHA

MIDDLE May at Istamboul!
Eastern breezes blowing cool
From the distant Asian shore,
Ruffling water like the oar.
Sunlight in an amber flood,
Roses swelling in the bud;
Doves above on drowsy wing,
Every mosque roof glimmering.
Birds in brambly gardens old
Piping from the jasmine spray;
Everything aglow with gold, —
Istamboul in middle May!

Istamboul in middle May!
See! the Sultan goes to-day
To his favorite mosque, and there
Will he pass an hour in prayer.
What a throng his coming waits
By the stately palace gates!
Hither have they madly pressed,

Stealthy thief and beggar pest;
Here are jostled, man to man,
Greek and grave Armenian;
Here the Jew receives a blow
From his ancient Roman foe;
And with sullen brows and murk,
Frowns on all the ruling Turk.

Arms at rest, along the way
Stands a statuesque array;
File on serried file is seen,
Turbaned with the sacred green;
And as far as eye can view,
Bayonets of steely blue
Catch the midday sun, and throw
Back the scintillating glow.
Yonder marble mosque is where
Goes the Sultan for his prayer;
Yonder carpet fine is spread
For his royal feet to tread;
And this guardian throng must wait
Till he signs to ope the gate.

While the halting moments pass,
Comes with ringing clink of glass

One whose figure, tall and thin,
Bends beneath a water-skin.
He has caught a curious eye;
"Buy!" he cries, "*Howadji*, buy!"
"*Moya Täib?*"[1] we reply.
Suddenly his dark face shines,
Softening all its furrowed lines,
And a stream, long, long up-pent,
Has enthusiastic vent.
We of Anglo-Saxon birth,
Wanderers on alien earth,
By this Arab-Ishmael
Are entranced as by a spell,
While this story glibly slips
From Mustapha's bearded lips;—

"Time agone" (thus opes his tale),
"In a Nubian desert vale
With my people did I dwell
By a sweet oasis well.
There was goodly pasture here
Through the circling of the year;
Fruit we plucked from palm and fig,
And the grain grew ripe and big
Twice in every twelve-month's space,

[1] Is the water good?

In our lonely dwelling-place.
Here, to cheer each fleeting hour,
Smiled on me my desert flower;
Oh, what happiness was mine
In that land of glad sunshine!

"Once as joyfully I rode
Backward to our fair abode,
From a pilgrimage afar
To the gates of gray Gondar,
Down upon me, fierce of mien,
Swooped a band of Bedoueen,
As from haunted heights of rock
On some laggard of the flock
Hungry vultures swoop. In vain
Did I spur along the plain;
I must yield or die! — and then
Flashed across my wildered ken
One swift thought of her, my flower, —
Solace of my every hour.
I could not, with unchanged breath,
Look upon the face of death,
So I yielded, and was borne
Far away to pine and mourn, —
Far away a slave, and sold
For the base Egyptian gold.

"Never did I seem to fret
Over tasks my master set,
For within my bosom's night
Hope had fixed her star of light.
Daily did I watch and long
To escape the captive throng;
Week on weary week wore by,
And no less a slave was I;
Till a midnight revel deep
Laid on all a leaden sleep,
When, with soft and eager tread,
Far into the dark I fled,
Blindly wandered until morn
In the gloomy east was born.
Then, as day was lit with flame,
To a soldier's camp I came, —
In the ranks a man had died;
'You shall fill his place!' they cried.
Three long years! ah, three long years!
To my eyes sprang bitter tears;
Thinking of the days to be,
Mine was speechless misery.

"Soon we sailed away, and where
Old Esh-Shâm[1] lies, blossom-fair,

[1] Damascus.

'Mid her gardens, sweet with song,
Slothfully we tarried long.
Yet again we sailed, and here
Came, at dawning of the year.
I had earned release at last;
But my joy was overcast.
How could I my native shore
Gain with such a scanty store?
Hence behold the trade I ply, —
With my dripping water-skin
Threading ever out and in
Through the throng with ceaseless cry,
'Water, oh, sweet water, buy!'

"You, *Howadji*, you who know,
All the story of my woe;
Know my long and lorn exile
From the land where flows the Nile,
From the one who waits in vain
While the warm moons wax and wane,
Grant me gracious aid, and make
Kindly gift for her sweet sake!"

Such the moving tale we hear,
Hearkening with charmëd ear;

Honesty we seem to trace
In his grave, uplifted face,
And we salve his checkered palm
With the universal balm.
Joy illumines his sunken eyes, —
Then a Greek anear us cries :
"He is called '*The sire of lies!*'"
Turn we toward Mustapha — Gone!
Like the filmy mist at dawn,
Faded, vanished from the day.

Blare the trumpets, roll the drums ;
'T is a glorious display.
Shouts the throng : "The Sultan comes!"
Istamboul in middle May!

E-LIM-IN-AH-DO.

'T WAS in the bazaars of the Smyrniotes
That we heard the lingering call,
With its mellow, musical, bell-like notes,
And its rhythmic rise and fall.
It soared o'er the camel-driver's shout,
And the bale-bent porter's angry flout, —
"*O—O*
E-lim-in-ah-do!"

There were the figs of Omoorloo,
Large and luscious and bursting ripe;
And from a café near there blew
The tempting scent of the water-pipe;
But Tireh's grapes would have hung in vain
Upon the vines had we heard that strain, —
"*O—O*
E-lim-in-ah-do!"

Amber, clear as a prisoned ray
Of the morning sunlight, was forgot;

Rugs, rich with the hues of dying day,
  From the looms of Persia, lured us not.
While the motley Smyrna world swept by,
We hung on the sound of the witching cry, —
"*O—O*
E-lim-in-ah-do!"

Then out of the jostling crowd he came,
  With his crook-necked flask and his clink of glass;
As keen of eye and supple of frame
  As a Lydian pard we saw him pass, —
Saw him pass, and above the roar
Caught the lilt of his call once more, —
"*O—O*
E-lim-in-ah-do!"

Who can measure melody's power?
  It sways the soul with the same strange spell
On lovely lips in a lady's bower,
  Or those of a vagrant Ishmael.
And still floats back, with its thrilling bars,
The strain from the Smyrniote bazaars, —
"*O—O*
E-lim-in-ah-do!"

ON AN ANTIQUE LAMP

DEFT was the patient artisan
  Who moulded thee in such a way
That thou hast long outlasted man,
  Thy brother, built of frailer clay.

Dim ages since for mortal eyes
  The purple dark thou didst illume ;
But they, these fleeting centuries,
  Have known the light beyond the tomb.

Forever quenched thy flaring fire,
  And yet, to us, thou seem'st to cast
The ghost-flame of some dead desire
  From out the vistas of the past.

SUNRISE ON THE ÆGEAN

WESTWARD proudly was our vessel standing
'Neath the starry zenith calm and cold,
When the light lines, one by one expanding,
Streaked the east with bars of burnished gold;
O'er the bosom of the deep behind us
In a molten flood the colors flowed,
For a moment did the glory blind us,
With such radiance it glowed.

Rosy were the ripples that ran after
Where our prow a gentle furrow made;
Snowy sea-gulls seemed with wingëd laughter
O'er our heads to hover, unafraid.
Amethystine grew the mist banks hoary
That on Zea's fertile fig-slopes lay,
And the templed Sunium promontory
Flushed beneath the sunrise ray.

Half did we expect to see, back-flinging,
  Some great altar's sacrificial fire,
Half did we expect to hear, far-ringing,
  Clear-toned voices of some matin choir; —
Such as might have swelled in song sonorous,
  Welcoming the mariners of yore,
Strophe answering strophe in full chorus,
  Wind-borne from the rocky shore.

Then from out his Orient chamber lightly
  As a lover leaped the sun in air;
Under his divine caresses brightly
  Blushed the earth to know he found her fair.
And it seemed to us, with ardor burning,
  Watching how the land grew glad with morn,
That we were as wanderers returning
  To the clime where we were born.

And the while our hearts with swift pulsation
  Bounded as our barque beneath her sails,
Cried we with ecstatic emulation
  Greeting to the sunny Attic dales;
Greeting to the mountain peaks uplifting
  In the drifting hyacinthine haze,
Greeting to the silvery sands and shifting,
  Greeting to the flowery ways.

You may wander all the wide world over,
  See the sunrise kindle where you will, —
Never, though you be a life-long rover,
  Will it thrill the heart with such a thrill,
Flood the being with such rapt emotion,
  Fill the soul with such celestial peace,
As when first o'er the Ægean ocean
  It sublimes the hills of Greece!

NIGHT ON THE ACROPOLIS

NIGHT and no cloud,
But the great glory of the Grecian moon
Above us, and around us her pure light,
Making us dream of June
In lands where yet the winds are harsh and
loud,
And snow-drifts still are white
In shaded woodland nooks afar from sight.

But June is with us here, or more than June;
For saw we not to-day,
Where sweeps the plain from Megara away
To the brown sands that beach her crescent bay,
Mowers that swung the scythe and sung in
tune,
And laughed across the wheat
To maidens sweet?
And now
The soft Ægean breeze that soothes the brow
Has happy hints of summer largess, blown

From that luxuriant zone
Where fruits hang crimson on the drooping
bough.

Ay! here is all a summer night can give,
Save regal roses and the nightingale;
And who, the leafy season long, would live
With ear wide-oped to Philomela's tale?
Or who would always find
The rich rose-attar spilled upon the wind?

Athens is Greece; and where is Athens' heart,
That throbs immortal, if it be not here?
The very dust is sacred, being a part
Of her great bosom. Every chiseled stone,
Each base, each arch, each pillar, placed or
prone,
To those who bow at Freedom's shrine is
dear.
Not less do they revere
This mighty rock who hold to Beauty's worth
In fusing thoughts of higher, grander things
Into the baser minds of earth;
For here, with heaven-plumëd wings,
Had Love of Beauty birth.

Do not the wraiths of the great gods of old,
Intangible, impalpable as air,
Here hover in their dumb, divine despair?
And what a grandeur shines
From their downthrown and desecrated shrines!
Behold, behold,
How, with imperious majesty of might,
Against the vast, moon-flooded wall of night,
The shattered shafts that were the Parthenon
Loom large upon the sight!
How flawless once the fluted columns shone,
When, with grave chant and sacerdotal rite,
Before the unpolluted altars came
From th' Eleusinian fane, in windings long,
A garland-crownëd throng
To render homage unto Ceres' name!
Still are there pilgrim feet, and still will be
While toward the sapphire gulf of Phaleron
And purple Salamis,
O'er Attica's warm meadows steadfastly
Frowns the stern brow of the Acropolis.
Though the Greek gods be dead,
The best their worship fostered still abides,
Eternal as the unfathomed ocean's tides,
Or as the hallowed soil whereon we tread.

We may not linger till the night wax old,
But, ere we turn to go,
Shall we not greet clear Hesper rising slow
Above Hymettus, looming black and bold?
Whence the celestial brilliance of yon star
That no moon-glory pales?
Surely above the violet vales afar,
On shores where surge the occidental seas
In billowy symphonies,
It never shone in such mysterious wise!
Drink in, O wondering eyes,
The starlight and the moonlight on these dales,
And on the sacred mountain-tops that rise
To sacred skies!
Reach out, O yearning soul, be drenched in light!
Melt into, mingle with, the soul of night!
This is thy Greece; thy dearest dream is won;
Thou standest on thy hope's supremest height,
Within the shadow of thy Parthenon!

THE TETTIX

DEWY and fragrant was the twilight falling
  Upon the wide sweep of the Argive plain,
But, from the oleander copses calling,
  No night-bird voiced its immemorial pain.

Yet, clear and sweet, harmonious and winning, —
  Bar intermingling with melodious bar, —
The tireless tettix with its violining
  Filled all the sundown silence near and far.

And we, who loved the blithe note of the cricket
  Beside the hearth when autumn days were bleak,
Hearing this home-like sound from mead and thicket,
  Felt in our hearts a kinship for the Greek.

ORACLES

BEFORE the birth-song of the Galilean
Thrilled through the spheres afar,
Long ere the echo of that sweet peace pæan
Was borne from star to star,

Men sought from prophets, priests, and statues graven,
To gain some gleam of light
That should illume the future's pathway, paven
With shadows dark as night.

Far in the heart of Libyan deserts arid
Was Ammon's altar reared;
And long and patiently the pilgrims tarried
To list the voice they feared.

The laureled Pythian priestess of Apollo,
From hills that Delphi crown,
Inspired by breathings from her cave's black hollow,
Sent her weird visions down.

Dodonian oaks, through whom low tongues seemed crying
To every wandering breeze,
Drew, by their power of wondrous prophesying,
Strange folk far over seas.

Happy were they who dreamed of no deceiving,
Whate'er the worshiped shrine,
Who lived undoubting lives out, still believing
In tokens sibylline.

Shall we, who bow before the one eternal
And gracious Godhead, hold
In scorn what they deemed sacred in those vernal
Sweet Grecian days of old?

Ah, no, for while its lustrous light outflinging,
Clear gleams the morning star,
The vocal trees, the free birds' rapturous singing,
Will be oracular!

A GREEK PASTORAL

THE sky is like a sea without a shore;
Both fruit and blossom gleam upon the lime;
The bees are murmurous in the fragrant thyme,
Gathering honey for their winter store.
Yon gentle slope is like a flowery floor,
With lavish cistus bloom as white as rime;
Among the boulders gray the spry goats climb,
And up the air the swift-winged swallows soar.

It is the drowsy hour when Pan of old
Dreamed in the shade, when shepherds strayed abroad
And wooed with song, nor watched the young lambs feed;
Sleep still enthralls the vision-haunted god,
While clear as ever lover piped, and bold,
Young Thyrsis pipes upon his oaten reed.

A TEAR BOTTLE

For Daphne were the tear-drops shed
  With which this tiny urn was wet,
The while they wove about her head
  Sweet sprays of Delphian serpolet?

And did they place it in her tomb, —
  This sad libation of their tears, —
The maids whose fair cheeks wore the bloom
  Of tenderly unfolding years?

And did he come, the one whose heart
  In hers responsive love had found,
And stand, with quivering lip, apart
  From all the mourners gathered round?

"A figment of the brain," you say,
  "An idle rhymer's idle rhyme;"
And yet how grief can sweep away
  The shadowy barriers of time!

HONEY OF HYMETTUS

Did you dream last year that we
E'er should tread the myrtled lea,
    E'er should taste the amber honey
Of the Hymettean bee?
  Yet to-day we blithely rove
  Through this gnarlëd Grecian grove,
    While below us, broad and sunny,
Booms the blue Ægean Sea.

Yonder, purple in the wide
Lustrous light of noonday-tide,
    Lie the flowery reaches fragrant
Where the nectar-gatherers bide;
  Cyclamen, anemone,
  Asphodel a-swinging free,
    Do they drain, each wingëd vagrant,
Haunting all the long hillside.

Vainly, vainly, did we seek
For the splendor of the Greek,

For some remnant of the glory
Of the mythic time antique.
Now the Parthenon is rent,
Th' Eleusinian fane is shent,
And Ilissus, great in story,
Is the ribbon of a creek.

But thy heights, Hymettus, yield
All the largess they concealed
When the warrior faced the foemen,
With the spear and with the shield.
This they could not bear away,
Those that made thy land a prey, —
The Venetian, Turk, and Roman,
Pilfering thy fertile field.

Though the Greeks that wander now
Underneath the laurel bough,
By the shore on sands Ægean,
With a louder praise endow
Honey stilled by island bees
On the slopes in middle seas, —
Honey drained from blossoms Zean,
Bright on many a mountain brow;

Yet will we with fervor sing,
Thine our lyric offering,
Golden bounty of Hymettus,
Luscious treasure of the spring!
Not for us the nectar bland
Of the fruitful island-land;
Swell the olden greetings; let us
Strike anew the Orphic string!

Join the chorus, ye who will!
"Honey of Hymettus hill,"
Dew divine through unseen portal
Poured the chalice-blooms to fill!
What rare opulence is ours!—
Essence of Elysian flowers,
Sacred to the bards immortal,
We will hold it sacred still!

A FERN FROM THE PIERIAN SPRING

THIS fragile fern-frond has for me
  The illusive charm that some songs hold,
For it once heard the melody
  Of that famed fount of old.

The stern gray walls are wasted now,
  That saw the wide gulf's azure span,
And riots the wild fig-tree bough
  O'er shrines Corinthian.

Yet still the spring wells, cool and clear,
  As in far Sophoclean time, —
A draught divine, and to the ear
  A silver rill of rhyme.

Here was the Muses' fair demesne,
  And still they tend the crystal urn,
Keeping the love of song as green
  As this frail frond of fern.

MOONRISE OVER SALAMIS

BACK from o'erthrown Corinthian shrines we came;
The day had died in flame;
The purple mountains one by one grew black
As some dense thunder-wrack,
And like a meteor among the stars
Flamed the red war-orb, Mars.

With sweet monotony of silvern sound
Did the warm waves rebound, —
The fond, dark waves caressing the curved shore.
There was no noise of oar,
But from the olives, rapturous notes and swift
Did one lone night-bird lift.

Then o'er the isle's dim brow did we behold
A radiant blade of gold,
That grew by gradual increase, till it hung
In middle air, and flung

From its resplendent arc such lines of light
That night was no more night.

This moon-bright isle, this moon-bright bay-sweep, — this
Was glorious Salamis,
Where Persia's boasted pomp of empire fell
Sheer to defeat's grim hell;
And where, heroic o'er the rout-strewn seas,
Towered grand Themistocles.

Dimmed by the magic moonlight, from its throne
Paler the war-star shone;
No serried oar-banks did we see arise,
We heard no battle-cries;
Yet vague the breathing present seemed to us, —
The past was luminous.

We marked the fragrant smoke of sacrifice
Mount to the moonlit skies;
We felt the great heart-gratitude that laid
Its touch on youth and maid; —
May we not thus re-live, in joys and woes,
Our earlier lives, — who knows?

A SHEPHERD'S CROOK

NOT on the hills of old,
In a shaggy-haired capote,
Did he tend the sheep and goat,
And drive them into the fold
With the sturdy crook I hold.
Flesh and blood is he now,
Bronzed by the sun and strong
As his nimble-footed flock;
And he loves the mountain's brow,
The gorge and the beetling rock,
The brook and the wild bird's song;
For he comes of the hardy stock
That roamed over Arcady
When the Persian crossed the sea.

Wave but this as a wand, —
This crook of the shepherd wight, —
And sudden from out the sight
The Near will waver and fail;
Now, in the changing light,

See, there rises a land
Arched with a sapphire bright,
Billowed with hill and vale!
"Arcady 's dead," you say;
Lo! we are there to-day.

Here, with his sheep around,
Is the shepherd tawny-faced,
With his leggings tightly laced,
And his russet cape awry,
And his lithe waist girdle-bound;
Here is ore from the sky,
Fresh from the mines of the sun, —
An open asphodel bell;
And there, where the waters run
Dancing down to the dell,
The myrtles change their sheen
From silver to tremulous green;
And she, — she walks by my side,
Like a goddess steadfast-eyed.

We have our Arcadies — all;
They spring at the charmëd call.
A ribbon, a rose, a ring,
Some half-remembered rhymes,

To the empty heart will bring
The vision of golden times ;
A wafture of faint perfume,
A ray through a darkened room,
The merry laugh of a brook,
The wave of a shepherd's crook ;—
Come, then, away with me
To the land of Arcady !

HYMN OF THE MORNING

I.

Of old,
When all the east was lit with Morn's first gold,
And slumbering Thebes awoke,
And splendors through her pillared porches broke, —
Torches of crimson, tongues of amethyst,
That arch and column kissed, —
When burst these glories, then
A song of aspiration,
A chant of inspiration,
The mouth of Memnon spoke unto the sons of men.

II.

The wakening desert heard,
And that resplendent bird,
The pink flamingo, flying fleet and far;
And drowsing at the oar,
The chained slave, laboring sore,

Whom night had blessed not from her restful
star.
Through every door
That sound its summons bore;
"Arise!" it said, — a mighty trumpet call
To one and all;
A call to breast the strife,
And struggle foremost in the van of life;
Not for the low and base,
But to exalt the race.

III.

Memnon is silent now,
And Thebes stands spectral on the desert's
brow.
But we,
Beyond the unsounded sea,
Hear Dawn's memnonic voice from stream and
tree,
From upland, vale, and lea.
Hark! how they greet the morn,
As though a god were born! —
The patriarchal poplar, spiring high,
The spreading elm, a spraying fount of shade,
The stanch maternal maple, great of thigh,

The arrowy pine, as sinewy as a blade.
Theirs is the rousing call that Memnon made;
The roving winds are heralds of their speech,
But the deep truths they teach
On dull souls fall with meaning lightly weighed.

IV.

Long, long ago,
A poet's prophet soul,
Where ocean's waters roll
Round Albion's cliff-girt isle with tireless flow,
Proclaimed a newer Orient should be
Unshackled, free,
Between the eastern and the western sea,
Where all the arts
Should flower in human hearts, —
Religion, science, song, —
And want should die, and sanguine war, and
wrong.

V.

Look forth on every hand!
Here lies the Morning-land,
The grand, the new!
No sunset clime is this,

But Dawn's supernal apotheosis;
Yet has indeed the prophecy come true?

VI.

They hearkened not of yore to Memnon's call,
And lo! above their fall
The obliterating desert sands are blown,
And the wild dogs make moan.
They reared themselves huge idols; set their store
On pleasure and the siren light of gold;
The power of place was more
Than righteousness. The great was bought and sold,
Till Justice shrank abashed before the base and bold.
Still others saw, and heard
The sunrise-spoken word,
But heeded not, and now
They are as Thebes upon the desert's brow.

VII.

While eastern skies are grandly luminous,
Shall we not list the mighty call to us?
Great Memnon-nature calling through her rills,

Her everlasting hills,
Her choral forest aisles,
Her billowy meadow miles,
Her soaring birds, her blooms,
Her colors, her perfumes,
Her winds, her showers, her waves,
Her echo-breathing caves?

VIII.

It is the Morning-spirit that uplifts;
Turn toward her!
Yearn toward her!
Not the cloud-banks, but the azure rifts;
Not the shadow, but the glow;
Not the stagnance, but the flow;
The lofty, not the low, —
Such be the creed
To meet our need.

IX.

As the lotus on Nile's broad bosom longs deep for the sky,
As papyrus reeds lean to the current that murmureth by,

As the citron leaves tremble to songward when
nightingales sing,
As the camel alone in the desert is drawn to-
ward the spring,
As the foal of the Nedjidee Arab turns, sleep-
less and sure,
Toward the path whence its mother will leap
with its cry for a lure,
Let us face toward the Morn, for the breath of
the Morning is pure!

X.

And let us climb upon aspiring feet
The soaring heights, and be the first to greet
The apocalyptic outburst that sublimes
The wide unrolling of our clime of climes!
The vales are lovely, but to him who stands
Above the thralldom of the lower lands
The fairest revelations are made known;
Yet not to scale these earthly heights alone
Our powers should bend, but heights of mind
and soul,
If we would make of man a perfect whole;
Upon those sacred summits far more clear

The penetrating rays of Truth appear.
Her beams will conquer; those upon the height
Should be the strenuous bearers of the light,
Dispelling empty phantoms of the night.

XI.

All great souls gone,
  How they faced the Morning,
    And wrought with might for the Truth and
      God!
They welcomed the Dawn,
  And the cry of warning,
    And smote at wrong with a cleaving rod.
They tended the fires
  Upon Progress' altar,
    And theirs was the zeal that the martyrs
      made;
In their high desires
  There was none to falter
    With the lifted voice, or the lifted blade.

XII.

Then cry, O Memnon, cry!
Exhort and prophesy,
That we may keep our Morning-heritage

So pure from age to age
That no obscuring blight
May dim its widening light,
But it may shine, of lands the fairest born,
When bursts o'er earth the everlasting Morn.

www.ingramcontent.com/pod-product-compliance
Lightning Source LLC
LaVergne TN
LVHW021422110826
845150LV00007B/2041